L
I
F
E
V
I
E
W
S

Published by Creative Education
123 South Broad Street, Mankato, Minnesota 56001
Creative Education is an imprint of The Creative Company

Art direction by Rita Marshall; Production design by The Design Lab

Photographs by Corbis (David Muench, NASA/Roger Ressmeyer, John Noble, Carl & Ann Purcell, William James Warren), The Image Finders (Rita Byron, Mark E. Gibson, Bruce Leighty, Werner Lobert), Tom Stack & Associates (J. Lotter Gurling, Brian Parker, Eric Sanford, Mark A. Stack, Therisa Stack, Ryan C. Taylor, TSADO/NASA/Tom Stack & Associates, TSADO/NOAA/Tom Stack & Associates), Weatherstock (J. Christopher, Warren Faidley, M. Laca, NOAA/NS)

Library of Congress Cataloging-in-Publication Data

Rotter, Charles.
Hurricanes / by Charles Rotter.
p. cm. — (LifeViews)
Summary: Briefly describes the characteristics of hurricanes and
how they are formed, highlighting the 1969 hurricane Camille.
ISBN 1-58341-020-1
1. Hurricanes—Juvenile literature. [1. Hurricanes.] I. Title. II. Series.
QC944.2 .R68   2002
551.55'2—dc21
                              2001047900

First Edition

2 4 6 8 9 7 5 3 1

STORMS OF THE SEA

HURRICANES

CHARLES ROTTER

HURRICANES represent a terrifying side of nature. Striking various areas around the globe, they have been wreaking havoc longer than people have been walking the earth. These immense **storms** batter the landscape with their fierce winds and torrential rains. The awful specter of **destruction** can haunt people for a long time—far longer than it takes to rebuild the actual damage done by the waves, wind, and rain.

Hurricanes have different names in different parts of the world. Only when they originate in the Atlantic Ocean or the eastern Pacific Ocean do we call them hurricanes. On the western Pacific,

Hurricanes are huge, violent storms.

off the coast of China, for example, they are called **typhoons**, from a Chinese phrase meaning "big wind." When they originate in the Indian Ocean, they are called **cyclones**. Australians probably have the most colorful name for hurricanes: they call the storms willy-willies.

Every hurricane, no matter what its name or where it occurs, is a type of weather disturbance known as a tropical cyclone. Usually about 300 to 400 miles (483–644 km) in diameter, the storms can generate winds exceeding 200 miles (322 km) per hour. This wind speed is part of the definition of a hurricane. If the wind speed is less than 75 miles (121 km) per hour, the storm does not qualify as a hurricane.

Tropical cyclones are caused by changes in the atmosphere, the layer of air that surrounds the earth. Photographed from space, the earth seems covered with still blue oceans and wispy white clouds. But this tranquil appearance is deceiving. The earth's atmosphere is very active, constantly moving and changing both its temperatures and its moisture patterns. These changes cause everything we call weather, including

From space, hurricanes look like giant spinning commas or pinwheels. Hurricane Hugo (right) hit the coast of South Carolina in 1989 with sustained wind speeds of more than 135 miles (217 km) per hour.

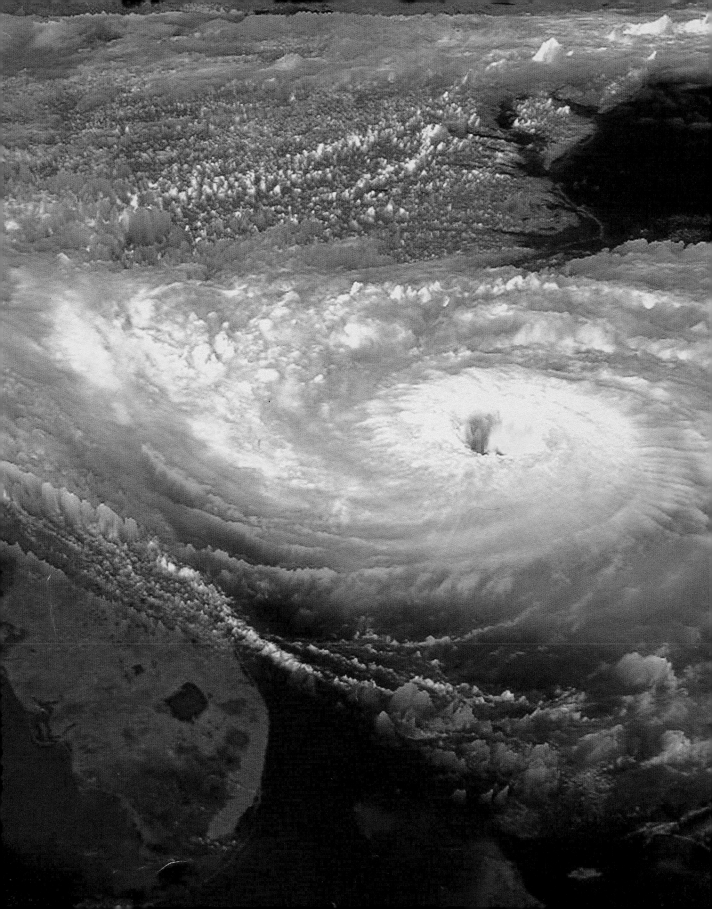

rain, snow, thunderstorms, tornadoes, and, of course, hurricanes. Even the most violent winds are just rapidly moving air.

The source that drives this air movement is the sun. As the earth orbits the sun, a great deal of light and heat shines down upon the planet. Some of this **energy** bounces back into space, but most of it is absorbed by the earth's surface. The greatest warming occurs near the **equator**, where the sun normally shines the brightest.

As the sun heats the earth's surface, it also heats the air in contact with that surface. The heated air expands and becomes lighter. Lighter air rises, just like the heated air that lifts a hot-air balloon. This creates an area called a low-pressure zone, where the air is less dense than the air that surrounds it. Such zones are also called **depressions**. When a mass of air is cool and dense, it forms a high-pressure zone.

A difference in air pressure causes air to flow from the higher pressure zone to the lower one to equalize the difference. This difference is known as the pressure-gradient, and the moving air is what we call **wind**. The wind does not move

Essentially, the sun is the source of all weather on Earth. Radiant energy, which is invisible to the naked eye, heats bodies of water and causes evaporation. The water vapor cools as it rises and forms clouds.

in a straight path. Instead, it flows at an angle to the pressure-gradient. This is due to the Coriolis effect, a phenomenon discovered in 1835 by French scientist Gaspard-Gustav de Coriolis. By mathematical calculations, Coriolis showed that a moving object's path on a rotating surface curves away from its original direction. This explains why a ball rolled across the surface of a spinning merry-go-round will move in a curve.

Similarly, air moving inward toward a depression moves in a circular path. This spiral of air is called a cyclone, a term invented by Captain Henry Piddington in the late 1830s. Piddington was studying storms off the coast of India when he noticed a whirling pattern in the clouds. He called the storms cyclones, from the Greek word *kyklon*, meaning "whirling around." Modern technology allows us to appreciate how good his choice of name was: now, when we use radar to map hurricanes or when we view them from space, we can easily see the whirling pattern.

Today, the term "cyclone" describes not just the storms in the Indian Ocean, but any mass of air spiraling in toward a

Satellite images help meteorologists track a hurricane's movement, measure its size, and calculate its intensity. Before 1960, hurricane prediction relied on ships, island weather stations, and coastal radar—all of which were imprecise.

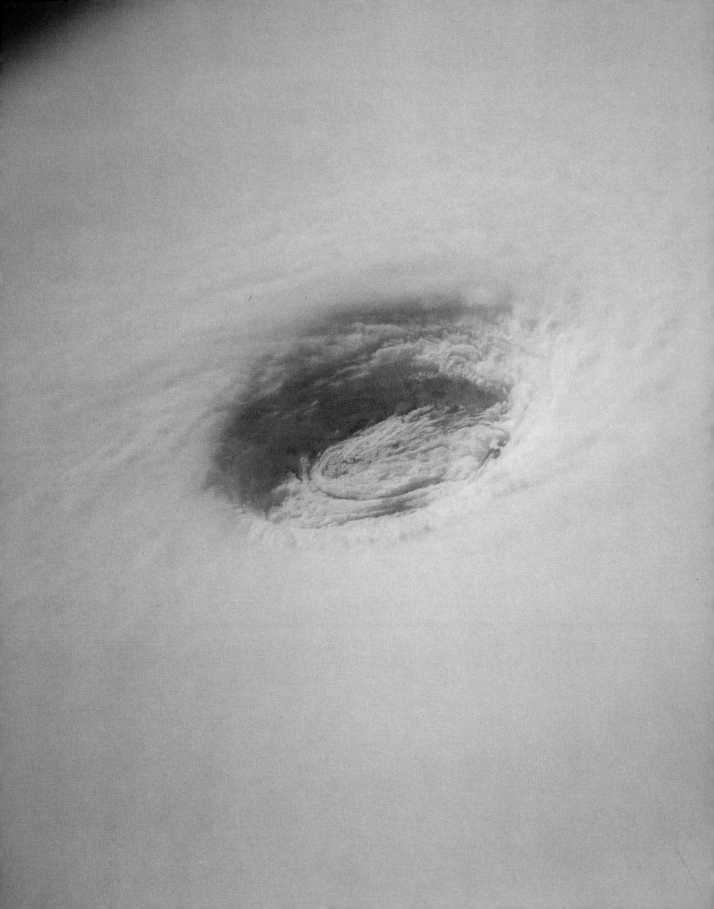

depression. A **tornado** can be called a cyclone. In the Northern Hemisphere, cyclones turn counterclockwise; in the Southern Hemisphere, they turn clockwise.

A hurricane is a special type of cyclone called a tropical cyclone. Tropical cyclones form over warm seas, far from land. The ocean surface must be warm enough to provide the energy a cyclone needs—at least 80 °F (27 °C). At these temperatures, warm, moist air constantly rises from the surface of the water to create low-pressure regions over the open ocean. Cool, denser air spirals into the depression, creating the cyclone wind pattern. Only about 1 in 10 of these tropical depressions will attain the energy needed to become a full-fledged tropical cyclone, or hurricane.

Appearing both above and below the equator, tropical cyclones originate between 5 and 20 degrees **latitude**. Within five degrees of the equator, the Coriolis effect is too small to provide the spin needed to build large storms; outside of 20 degrees, the water isn't warm enough. After forming, the storms tend to move in a westward direction. This means that

Warm, moist air rising from the seas fuels hurricanes.

land at the western edges of oceans is much more threatened by hurricanes than land at the eastern edges.

The strong winds of a hurricane spiral inward toward the center of the storm, called the eye. Ranging from 5 to 25 miles (8–40 km) wide, the eye of a hurricane is calm and almost windless. This calm can create an extremely hazardous situation: thinking that the storm has passed, people may relax and leave shelters. But the danger is far from over—it is actually only moments away from its peak.

Hurricanes can cause incredible amounts of damage when they move onto land. Storm-swollen waves do the most harm. The low-pressure center at the eye of a hurricane can cause the sea level to rise several feet. Driven by the violent wind, the waves batter the shore and flood low-lying communities near the coast.

As the warm, moist air of a hurricane rises and condenses, the storm also generates intense rainfall, which makes the flooding even worse as the storm passes onto land. When

Atlantic hurricane season runs from June through the end of November. It reaches its peak in August and September, when longer daylight hours allow the sun more time to heat the ocean surface and the air above it.

moisture condenses into water, heat energy is released. The massive rainfall from a hurricane releases a great deal of heat energy, which continues to drive the storm on land even though it has been deprived of its main source of energy (the rising moist air of the tropical seas). But this new source of **power** is limited, and while over land, the hurricane steadily weakens. It can regain its strength only if it moves out over the open water. Otherwise, it will continue to weaken until it is reduced to an ordinary tropical depression.

In 1969, one of the mightiest hurricanes in the modern history of the Western Hemisphere lashed the Atlantic coast of the United States. First spotted by a weather satellite on August 5, **Hurricane Camille** formed near the Cape Verde Islands, off the northwest coast of Africa. The storm grew in size until it reached full hurricane proportions, then headed west across the Atlantic Ocean. By August 12 it was assaulting Puerto Rico and still growing in intensity.

Weather **forecasters** watched Camille closely and tried to predict its path, which was erratic. They sent out aircraft to

Hurricanes can cause an incredible amount of property damage, especially in heavily populated coastal areas. One of the costliest hurricanes in U.S. history was Hurricane Andrew in 1992. Damage costs exceeded $25 billion.

locate and study the hurricane, hoping to warn people in its path as well as to obtain scientific knowledge of the storm. As Camille passed near the western tip of Cuba, timely **warnings** by forecasters saved many people in that country from injury or even death. Camille then headed for the United States—but where would it strike?

Hurricane experts worked furiously to answer that question. They collected every bit of information they could from planes, **satellites**, and ground observations. Then they fed this information into computers. The computer models predicted that Camille would strike the southern part of Florida. But computer forecasting was new in 1969, and the forecasters' own experience with similar storms made them treat this prediction with caution. Many of them felt that the hurricane would strike the northwest coast of Florida instead. On the morning of August 16, the National Hurricane Center in Miami issued a conservative warning based on these conclusions. The warning stretched from St. Marks, Florida, to Biloxi, Mississippi. The next day, scientists observed erratic

As the eye of the hurricane approaches land, fierce winds ahead of it drive tons of water ashore in great swells called storm surges. Damage can be especially great if the storm hits land at high tide.

changes in the behavior of Camille, causing them to extend their warning westward as far as New Orleans, Louisiana.

During this time, Camille had been sitting off the coast, growing in strength. By the morning of August 17, it became clear that Camille probably would avoid Florida altogether and instead would assault the coast somewhere between Louisiana and Mississippi. The Hurricane Center issued strong warnings, and many people wisely **evacuated** the coastal areas, heading inland to safety. Those who ignored the warnings, or waited until it was too late, regretted their decisions. Some paid for this mistake with their lives.

The storm charged the Mississippi coast near the city of Gulfport. With winds up to 190 miles (306 km) per hour, Camille knocked down telephone poles, powerlines, and nearly everything else in its path. Residents of the storm-ravaged communities feared for their lives. Structures near the coast were the hardest hit. The buildings not destroyed by the wind were deluged by a **tidal surge** 25 feet (7.6 m) high. Many of the people in these buildings were killed.

Although a storm surge is perhaps the most destructive part of a hurricane, other dangers, such as torrential rains, flooding, intense lightning, and high winds, may be felt far inland—sometimes hundreds of miles from the coast.

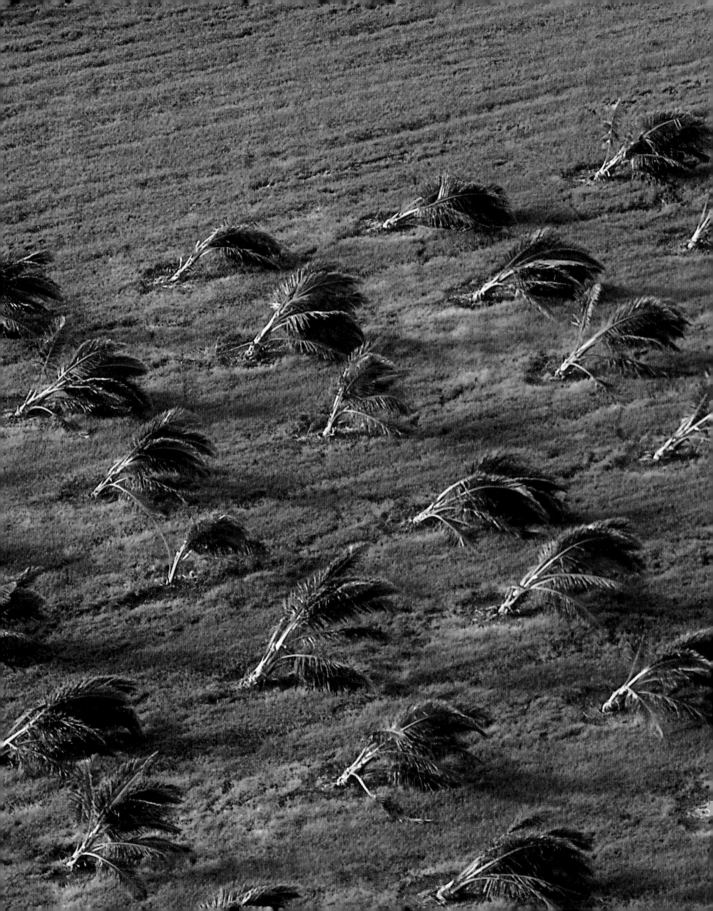

When the storm was finally over, the **death toll** was 330, and the damage to property was estimated at more than $1.5 billion. While the forecasters' initial predictions had been inaccurate, their final warnings still allowed hundreds, perhaps thousands, of people to seek **refuge** in time to save their lives. Who knows how much greater the death toll would have been without the efforts of these scientists?

Camille was one of the most powerful hurricanes ever to hit the United States. Yet the death toll from some other tropical cyclones, both in North America and in many other parts of the world, has been much greater. In 1737, a storm whipped across the southern coast of India, bringing waves and tidal surges that drowned an estimated 300,000 people. Even in the United States, other storms have been much worse than Camille. In 1900, for example, a violent hurricane deluged the Texas city of Galveston, killing 6,000 people.

It is not necessarily the intensity of the storm that determines its deadliness. Rather, it is the **vulnerability** of the people in its path. This is why the predictions of hurricane forecasters

Downed trees are of little consequence compared to the number of fatalities a hurricane can cause. If a hurricane is particularly devastating, such as Camille, its name is "retired" and cannot be used for future storms.

are so important. With adequate warning, people can prepare to ride out the storm or flee it, resulting in great savings of both lives and property.

Scientists studying the weather today have better tools at their disposal than did the experts who tracked Camille. Modern supercomputers, sophisticated satellites, and more sensitive instruments have all improved the accuracy of weather forecasting. But scientists face serious challenges. Because the population is increasing in vulnerable areas, many hurricanes still cause terrible **devastation**. This makes the science of hurricane prediction even more important. As it continues to improve, many more thousands of lives around the world can be saved by timely and accurate warnings.

It is unlikely that we will ever be able to control the awesome **forces** that combine to produce hurricanes. Like earthquakes and volcanoes, hurricanes represent the untamable power of nature. Advances in science and technology may save us from them, but only by helping us to get out of their way.

Large waves and increasing clouds can signal stormy weather.

MEASURING AIR PRESSURE

A barometer is an instrument used to measure atmospheric pressure. The measurement helps forecasters predict the weather. When the air pressure increases (and the barometer rises), cool, clear days are usually in the forecast. When the air pressure decreases (and the barometer drops), warm, wet days may be on the way. These instructions will show you how to make your own barometer so you can track air pressure in your area.

You Will Need
- Scissors
- A balloon
- A small jar, such as a peanut butter jar
- A heavy rubber band
- An 8 1/2-inch by 11-inch (22 cm x 28 cm) piece of construction paper
- Tape
- A drinking straw
- Craft glue
- A pen

Building the Barometer
1. Cut the neck off the balloon and stretch the top over the mouth of the jar. Secure the piece in place with the rubber band. Make sure the entire mouth of the jar is airtight.
2. Depending upon the height of your jar, fold the piece of construction paper into thirds to create a triangular tube that is either 8-1/2 inches (22 cm) or 11 inches (28 cm) tall. (The top of the jar should be about level with the middle of the tube.) Tape the ends together.
3. Cut one end of the straw at an angle to create a point. Lay the straw across the mouth of the jar with the pointed end sticking out. Glue the uncut end of the straw to the center of the balloon piece.

4. Set the jar next to the construction paper tube in a place where they won't be disturbed. Make sure the straw doesn't touch the paper. Using your pen, mark on a flat side of the tube the exact place to which the straw points. This will be your starting point. The straw will move above and below this line as the air pressure rises and falls.

Observation

Check your barometer daily. When the air pressure is high, the outside air will press hard on the air in the bottle, and the point of the straw will point higher. When the air pressure lowers, the air inside the bottle will push up, and the point of the straw will go down. This could signal the approach of stormy weather.

The first mercury barometer was created in 1643 by an Italian physicist named Evangelista Torricelli. (Mercury is a heavy, liquid metal that is very sensitive to temperature and pressure changes.) Today, two types of barometers are used to measure atmospheric pressure: mercury and the less sophisticated aneroid (made without liquid). The barometer you just made is similar to an aneroid barometer. Weather prediction centers prefer mercury barometers because they are more accurate. Air pressure is measured in inches or millibars, with standard air pressure at sea level measuring about 29.92 inches of mercury or 1,103 millibars. The lowest air pressure ever recorded occurred in 1979 during a typhoon in the Pacific Ocean.

RATING WIND SPEED

Whirling at speeds of 75 to 180 miles (120–288 km) per hour, hurricane winds rate a 12 on the Beaufort Wind Force Scale, the highest rating possible. British Commander Francis Beaufort created this scale in 1805 as a way to systemize wind force measurements at sea. It was later adapted for wind effects on land. The rating system is based on subjective observations of nature. Although meteorologists today have more sophisticated, objective methods for measuring wind speed, many amateur weather watchers still use it. Try keeping your own weather journal and rate the daily wind speed in your area using the Beaufort Scale.

Force 0:   Calm. Trees are still.

Force 1:   Light air. Smoke drifts.

Force 2:   Slight breeze. Leaves rustle.

Force 3:   Gentle breeze. Leaves move all the time.

Force 4:   Moderate breeze. Flags flap.

Force 5:   Fresh breeze. Small trees sway.

Force 6:   Strong breeze. Large tree branches sway.

Force 7:   High wind. Whole trees sway.

Force 8:   Gale. Twigs break off trees.

Force 9:   Strong gale. Slight damage to buildings.

Force 10:   Very strong gale. Trees uprooted.

Force 11:   Storm. Widespread damage.

Force 12:   Hurricane. Severe and extensive damage.

LEARN MORE ABOUT HURRICANES

Canadian Hurricane Centre
c/o Maritime Weather Centre
45 Alderney Drive
Dartmouth, Nova Scotia
B2Y 2N6 Canada
http://www.ns.ec.gc.ca/weather/
    hurricane/chc.html

Federal Emergency Management Agency
P.O. Box 2012
Jessup, MD 20794
http://www.fema.gov/kids

The Hurricane Hunters Association
53rd Weather Reconnaissance Squadron
403rd Wing Division
701 Fisher Street
Keesler AFB
Biloxi, MS 39534
http://www.hurricanehunters.com

National Hurricane Center
11691 SW 17th Street
Miami, FL 33165
http://www.nhc.noaa.gov

National Weather Service
1325 East-West Highway
Silver Spring, MD 20910
http://www.nws.noaa.gov

USA Today.com
(online resource for current
    hurricane information)
http://www.usatoday.com/weather/hurricane

The Weather Channel
(check your local television listings)
http://www.weather.com

INDEX

Coastal wave conditions can be tracked by data buoys.